Green

Seeing Green All around Us

by Sarah L. Schuette

Reading Consultant:
Elena Bodrova, Ph.D., Senior Consultant,
Mid-continent Research for Education and Learning

Capstone press

Mankato, Minnesota

A+ Books are published by Capstone Press,
151 Good Counsel Drive, P.O. Box 669, Mankato, Minnesota 56002.
www.capstonepress.com

2 3 4 5 6 07 06 05

Library of Congress Cataloging-in-Publication Data
Schuette, Sarah L., 1976–
    Green: Seeing green all around us / by Sarah L. Schuette.
    p.cm.—(Colors)
    Summary: Simple text and photographs describe common things that are green, including plants
and traffic lights.
    Includes bibliographical references and index.
    ISBN-13: 978-0-7368-1468-3 (hardcover)   ISBN-10: 0-7368-1468-X (hardcover)
    ISBN-13: 978-0-7368-5065-0 (softcover pbk.)   ISBN-10: 0-7368-5065-1 (softcover pbk.)
    1. Green—Juvenile literature. [1. Green.] I. Title.
QC495.5 .S363 2003
535.6—dc21   2002000701

Created by the A+ Team

Sarah L. Schuette, editor; Heather Kindseth, designer; Gary Sundermeyer, photographer;
    Nancy White, photo stylist

A+ Books thanks Michael Dahl for editorial assistance.

Note to Parents, Teachers, and Librarians

The Colors series uses full-color photographs and a nonfiction format to introduce children to the world
of color. *Green* is designed to be read aloud to a pre-reader or to be read independently by an early reader.
Photographs and activities help early readers and listeners understand the text and concepts discussed.
The book encourages further learning by including the following sections: Table of Contents, Words to
Know, Read More, Internet Sites, and Index. Early readers may need assistance using these features.

Table of Contents

Green is hungry.
Green is big.

Green can grow on a branch or twig.

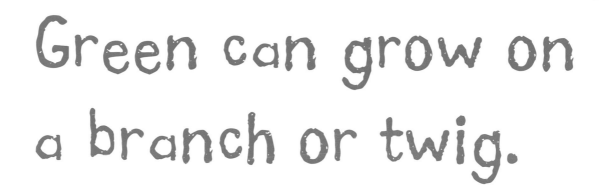

Light from the sun helps leaves stay green. Some leaves are always green. Other leaves turn red, orange, and yellow in fall.

Green beans also are called snap beans. Breaking a bean in half sounds like you are snapping your fingers.

Green is cooked.
Green is stewed.

Green gets munched.
Green gets chewed.

What do you and broccoli have in common? You both have heads. Heads of broccoli can be cut to make florets. You can have the hair on your head cut to make you look good.

Green iguanas are large lizards with scaly skin. Iguanas shed their skin in many pieces. The new skin is shiny and bright.

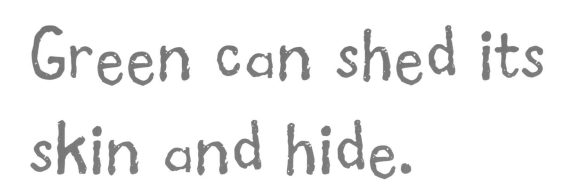

Green can shed its skin and hide.

Green snakes are long and legless. They have scales. Scales help snakes slither up trees to catch animals.

Green can slither.
Green can slide.

Other names for green are mint and forest. Green ice cream tastes fresh and minty.

Green is fresh.
Green is cool.

Green can write at home or school.

Ink is a colored liquid used for writing and printing. Ink comes in many colors.

Green says go to cars on the street.

Green lights tell drivers that it is safe to go. Traffic lights also help walkers know when to cross the street.

Green feels good under your feet.

Grass is green most of the year. It turns brown when the weather is cold. Some kinds of grass stay green all year.

Green is soft.
Green is dry.

Green towels soak up water. Towels dry you off after a shower or a bath.

Green things crawl.
Green things fly.

Making Green

Artists use a color wheel to know how to mix colors. Yellow, red, and blue are primary colors. They mix together to make secondary colors. Green, orange, and purple are the secondary colors they make. You can make green by mixing yellow and blue together.

You will need

3 clear glasses
water
blue and yellow food coloring

color wheel

1 Fill two of the glasses with water. Put two drops of blue food coloring in one glass.

2 Put two drops of yellow food coloring in the second glass.

3 Next, pour half of the blue water in the empty glass. Then, pour half of the yellow water in the same glass. What happens?

Words to Know

floret—the part of a broccoli head that looks like a small green flower

lizard—a reptile with a scaly body, four legs, and a long tail; iguanas are large lizards.

scale—one of the small pieces of hard skin on the body of a fish, snake, or other reptile; snakes and iguanas have scales.

shed—to let something fall off; snakes and iguanas shed their skin at least once a year.

slither—to slide and slip along the ground or up a tree; snakes slither to move because they do not have legs.

stew—to cook something for a long time

Read More

Granowsky, Alvin. *Colors.* My World. Brookfield, Conn.: Copper Beech Books, 2001.

Stone, Tanya Lee. *Living in a World of Green.* Woodbridge, Conn.: Blackbirch Press, 2001.

Whitehouse, Patricia. *Green Foods.* Colors We Eat. Chicago: Heinemann Library, 2002.

Internet Sites

FactHound offers a safe, fun way to find Internet sites related to this book. All of the sites on FactHound have been researched by our staff.

Here's how:
1. Visit *www.facthound.com*
2. Type in this special code 073681468X for age-appropriate sites. Or enter a search word related to this book for a more general search.
3. Click on the Fetch It button.

FactHound will fetch the best sites for you!

Index